Published by Knock Knock
Distributed by Knock Knock LLC
Venice, CA 90291
knockknockstuff.com

© 2015 Knock Knock LLC
All rights reserved
Knock Knock is a trademark of Knock Knock LLC
Made in China

ISBN: 978-1601067074
UPC: 825703-50044-8
10 9 8 7 6 5 4 3 2

Petsies

A PHOTO ALBUM OF ME, MY PET, AND I

KNOCK
KNOCK.®
VENICE, CALIFORNIA

A (Very) Brief History of the Petsie

15,000 B.C.
Paleolithic humans paint animals (horses, mammoths, and deer, to name a few) inside caves in Lascaux, France.

1434
The Arnolfini Portrait, a painting by Jan van Eyck, depicts a couple holding hands and a small terrier-like dog in the foreground.

1877
With multiple cameras, Eadweard Muybridge photographs running horses to prove that they lift all four feet while in motion.

2005-present
Websites like Cute Overload and I Can Has Cheezburger? compile photos of pets and other animals with silly captions.

2010
Instagram launches. Eventually, animal-only accounts appear, with dogs, cats, and even hedgehogs getting in on the action.

2010
Apple introduces the iPhone 4. The phone's front-facing camera lets users take self-portraits with pets without a mirror.

1906-1934

Cassius Marcellus Coolidge paints sixteen ads that depict anthropomorphic dogs for a publishing company. The ones with dogs playing poker become iconic.

1970

William Wegman photographs his Weimaraner, Man Ray. After Man Ray's death, Wegman continues to work with the breed, often dressing up the dogs.

1999

Oolong the rabbit becomes an Internet sensation after his owner Hironori Akutagawa poses him with various objects (most famously, a pancake) on his head.

2013

"Selfie" is the Oxford Dictionaries Word of the Year.

2013

Snapcat, an app that allows cats (and dogs) to take their own selfies, is created at a German hackathon.

2015

Knock Knock introduces Petsies: a Photo Album of Me, My Pet, and I.

5
Simple Tips for Taking Your Petsie

1. EXPECT THE UNEXPECTED

When you're photographing yourself, you control the situation. Add your pet into the mix, though, and who knows what could happen? Just be prepared to keep snapping pics—you might get a great shot.

2. THE FUR'S THE THING

Those days when Snuggles is fresh from the groomer and looking well-coiffed are cute—but so are those bad fur days. Plus, shaggy, unkempt animals always get a laugh.

3. SHOW THE NOT-SO-GOOD SIDE

While there's nothing cuter than a sleeping or sweetly posing pet, there's something to be said for capturing the moment when your animal has shredded all the toilet paper, or has left a trail of muddy prints.

4. ACCESSORIZE!

A well-placed prop—be it something that actually belongs to your pet (a toy) or not (a hat)—can make for a silly photo.

5. THE EYES HAVE IT

Your flash can make pets have crazy red or glowing eyes. For a more natural (and less scary) look, shoot in natural light, and skip the flash.

When the ruins of our modern society are discovered at some point in the distant future, chances are high that archeologists will determine an irrefutable truth about us: we love our cats, dogs, rats, hamsters, fish, bunnies, and other pets.

We are a nation of oversharers—informing friends, family, and sometimes strangers what we're wearing, eating, thinking, and doing at any and every given moment.

So in addition to snapping photos of our food, clothes, and sunsets with our camera-enabled smartphones, it only makes sense that we document ourselves—and our pets.

Why? Is it because, freed from the time and expense of developing film, we're all budding photographers? Or is it just that we really, really, really like our pets? Maybe it's simply a way to record that cute face Rover makes when he's tired. Whatever the reason, this photo album is a way to collect and keep those pet portraits worth saving.

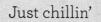

Just chillin'

Snuggling

Extreme close-up

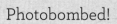

Photobombed!

Looking cute

#nofilter

Sleeping

Road trip!

In my spot

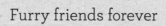

Furry friends forever

Happy!!!

Besties!

Posing

Sneaky

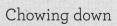

Chowing down

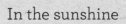

In the sunshine

Clean!

Dirty!

Playing hard

Uh-oh

So mad

Yawning

Dressed up

Hiding

With my favorite toy

#petstagram

Us!